# The Connection Cleanse

*Building your ultimate toolkit starts here*

## TRICIA SYBERSMA

HeartMath® is a registered trademark of Quantum Intech, Inc.
For all HeartMath® trademarks go to www.heart.com/trademarks

Print ISBN 979-8-9867969-4-9
Ebook ISBN 979-8-9867969-6-3

This publication is designed to provide accurate and authoritative information regarding the subject matter covered. It is sold with the understanding that the author is not engaged in rendering professional services. If legal, accounting, medical, psychological, or any other expert assistance is required, seek the services of a competent professional.

All imagery from Shutterstock.com
Design and layout by Rachel Rossano

# What's Inside

"If the only tool you ever
have is a *hammer*,
you may see every
problem as the same *nail*."

~ Abraham Maslow

# Which Experience are we in?

 **GRATITUDE**
*Experience Gratitude **for self**
and the world around you*

 **CONNECTION**
*Experience Connections **to self**,
community and beyond*

 **ACTION**
*Experience living **your life with awareness**
in the world around you*

# The Connection Cleanse Toolkit

## Invest in yourself!

Participating in *The Connection Cleanse*, *The Connection Experience*, and other programs offered through Gratitude~Connection~Action is an investment in yourself and the wealth of knowledge and wisdom that awaits discovery in your inner world.

This toolkit was designed to support your daily Connection Cleanse, as a companion program to *The Connection Experience* (see page 19).

Whether you need inspiration, options, or reminders, this toolkit will serve as your go-to resource for cleansing your internal space.

Keep it on hand to enhance your daily practice and deepen your connection with yourself and the world around you.

## Why cleanse connections?

Do you feel affected by everything around you?
Are you an empath or a deep feeler with a big heart?
Do you ever feel weighed down by all of the energy around you?

Feeling energy from self, your loved ones, and the world around you can be heavy. That's where the Connection Cleanse comes in!

*The Connection Cleanse* was created to help you learn how to become aware of your energetic connections, disconnect from depleting connections, strengthen uplifting connections, and empower yourself with choice.

**During the Cleanse, you will learn how to:**
- Become aware of energetic connections
- Disconnect from depleting connections
- Strengthen an uplifting connection
- Empowering ourselves with choice

> **Not only can you untangle this energy, but you can also choose your Connection or change it!**

# Clear Your Heart

TAKE SLOW AND DEEP BREATHS WHILE
RELAXING. DIRECT YOUR ATTENTION INWARD
TOWARDS YOUR HEART AREA.

# Breathwork

Working actively with your breath is an empowering technique that you can use anytime, anywhere. Enhance any of these with essential oils and/or gemstones.

## 1 Heart Breathing

Scan QR code to watch the video

Connect with the heart through breath.

- Breathe in and out with an intention and focus on the heart area.
- Brings about rapid physiological changes in your body.
- Commences an opening to heart energy; coveted in self-connection.

*Usage: Add this heart breath video into your daily routine where it feels right — try at the beginning or end of the day.*

## 2 Heart-Brain Connection Breath

Scan QR code to watch the video

Your heart has special neurons similar to those found in your brain. Connecting to these neurons is referred to as accessing your 'heart intelligence'.

This technique involves breathing in a way that creates a coherent heart rhythm, which in turn helps to regulate the brain and nervous system, and promotes emotional and physical balance.

*Usage: Join this short video and practice this breath when you feel anxious, stressed, or overwhelmed, to help you access your heart intelligence and find balance.*

## 3 Lung Meridian Tracing

Scan QR code to watch the video

Emotions can become stagnant in our bodies in various ways, and over time, all the connections that we form consciously and subconsciously may eventually infiltrate our system in a heavy way. Tracing our lung meridian can help to clear emotional energy and keep it flowing.

*Usage: Use this technique daily to maintain emotional flow as well as when needed.*

*If you have a crystal such as sunstone, celestine, or any favorite stone, grab it and join this short video on tracing your Lung Meridians!*

# Healing Through Sound

OPEN YOUR MIND AND LISTEN WITH YOUR HEART.

# Healing Music

Our senses connect us to the world, and sound is a powerful tool for healing. Tones, melodies, and frequencies can resonate through our mind, body, and spirit, organizing, informing, and structuring at a subtle level.

## 1 Connection Experience Soundtrack

This soundtrack was composed specifically for *The Connection Experience* journey. It is uplifting, cleansing, and unites the heart.
*Music by Dawn Hanley and production by Mark Caruana-Dingli*

## 2 Removing unconscious clutter - YouTube

This track helps to shake, shift, and dissolve the cobwebs of mental clutter. After listening, shift your mind to positive energy (like gratitude), and rewire your neurons to start working in a different direction.
*Music by DESNA and fielded by Sapien Medicine*

## 3 Binaural beats for connection - YouTube

The 852 Hz solfeggio frequency and beta binaural beats can help connect you to a higher awareness of yourself and your surroundings, as well as to divine sources. Listen to binaural beats with headphones on while relaxing.
*Music by DESNA and fielded by Sapien Medicine*

## 4 432Hz for connection to all - YouTube

This track is designed to help you connect to all. The 432Hz frequency is said to have a positive influence on the mind and body due to its relationship with our planet.
*Music by Angel Healing Music*

## 5 Let go of negative attachment

This track is designed to help you let go of negative attachments from anxiety, stress, overthinking, and depression.
*Music by Prabin Dangol from Meditation and Healing*

*Usage: Play any of the above tracks according to your needs and preferences.*
*Use them during your daily Connection Cleanse, meditation, or relaxation practice.*

# Harmonize with Nature

ENGAGE YOUR SENSES AND TAKE A DEEP BREATH TO CONNECT
WITH THE NATURAL WORLD.

# Essential Oils

Enhance your vibration and connect with nature's frequency through the intentional use of essential oils.

Therapeutic grade essential oils bring the therapeutic qualities of pure nature indoors for everyday use. They can help ground and protect your energy, clear your mind and heart, and uplift your spirit. However, not all essential oils are equal, so choose high-quality ones to avoid contaminants.

## 1  Basil Essential Oil

Basil is known for its ability to clear the heart and mind. Regular use of basil essential oil can help you build trust with yourself, allowing you to honor your needs and stay open-hearted in the process.

*Usage: Add 2-3 drops to your hands, rub them together, and inhale deeply. You can also apply the oil over the heart to help anchor into a heart-breathing routine. For a more targeted approach, apply the oil to specific points on the body that correlate to the organ and meridian associated with the element you want to support.*

## 2  Rosemary Essential Oil

Rosemary energizes the nervous system, uplifts the spirit, and enhances mental clarity. It can also help you maintain healthy boundaries so that you don't lose yourself in others.

*Usage: Add 2-3 drops to your hands, rub them together, and inhale deeply. You can also apply the oil over the heart to help anchor into a heart-breathing routine. For a more targeted approach, apply the oil to specific points on the body that correlate to the organ and meridian associated with the element you want to support.*

## 3  Vetiver Essential Oil

Vetiver has highly grounding properties, as its roots naturally grow very deep. It is also beneficial for highly sensitive individuals as it can help protect their energy from others.

*Usage: Add 2-3 drops to your hands, rub them together, and inhale deeply. You can also apply the oil over the heart to help anchor into a heart-breathing routine. For a more targeted approach, apply the oil to specific points on the body that correlate to the organ and meridian associated with the element you want to support.*

*For questions or assistance with essential oils, visit www.LetHealthFlow.ca*

# Resonate with Gemstones

HARNESS THE POWER OF NATURE'S TREASURES
FOR HEALING AND INSPIRATION.

# Gemstones

Connect with the intention and frequency of nature at your fingertips by incorporating gemstones into your self-care routine. You can also enhance your vibration by pairing them with essential oils.

Did you know that gemstones hold energy, frequency, and consciousness? Not only are they beautiful to have near you, but they also vibrate with healing energy that can help balance your energy.

## 1 Sunstone

Sunstone boosts your sense of self-empowerment and infuses you with worthiness, helping negative energies melt away, leaving you with a radiance of optimism and a positive attitude.

*Usage: Hold the palm stone safely and comfortably (depending on size) and use it to trace your meridians. Consider pairing with essential oils for an even more powerful experience.*

## 2 Celestine

Celestine helps you find your inner balance and perfect sense of peace. It's the perfect gemstone to use when connecting with your higher self, and the energy realms, such as angels.

*Usage: Hold the palm stone safely and comfortably (depending on size) and use it to trace your meridians. Consider pairing with essential oils for an even more powerful experience.*

*For questions or assistance with gemstones, visit www.LetHealthFlow.ca*

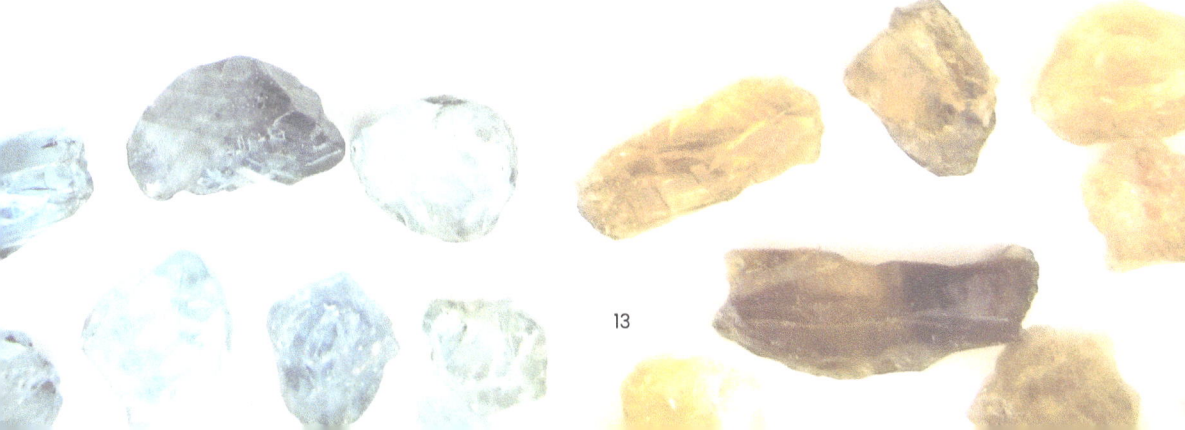

# Daily Check-In

USE THE POWER OF DAILY CHECK-INS TO
BUILD MOMENTUM AND ACHIEVE YOUR
GOALS, NO MATTER HOW SMALL.

# Your Daily Check-in

Track your progress and emotions. Use this check-in to record how you feel each day and add any notes that you like.

By taking a few minutes to check-in with yourself, you can build self-awareness, cultivate mindfulness, and stay motivated on your journey.

Whether you want to monitor your mood, track your habits, or reflect on your accomplishments, this daily check-in is your personal tool for growth and reflection.

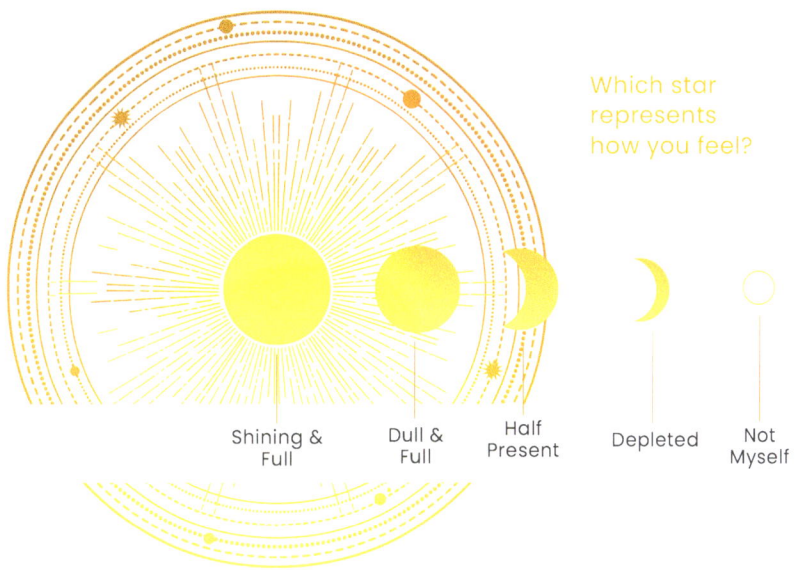

Which star represents how you feel?

| Shining & Full | Dull & Full | Half Present | Depleted | Not Myself |

## Day 1 ~ rating and notes

_____

_____

_____

_____

_____

_____

_____

_____

# Your Daily Check-in

Day 2 ~ rating and notes

_____
_____
_____
_____
_____
_____
_____

Day 3 ~ rating and notes

_____
_____
_____
_____
_____
_____
_____

Day 4 ~ rating and notes

_____
_____
_____
_____
_____
_____
_____

Day 5 ~ rating and notes

_____

_____

_____

_____

_____

_____

_____

_____

Day 6 ~ rating and notes

_____

_____

_____

_____

_____

_____

_____

_____

Day 7 ~ rating and notes

_____

_____

_____

_____

_____

_____

_____

_____

# Expand and Grow

DISCOVER A WORLD OF RESOURCES AND
TOOLS TO SUPPORT YOUR PERSONAL AND
PROFESSIONAL GROWTH JOURNEY.

# Expansion Options

This toolkit is not limited to just what we have listed. It is designed to expand and evolve with you. Here are a few more options to consider, and feel free to add any tools that you find beneficial for yourself.

### BRACELET

Bring in high-quality and ethically sourced gemstones that resonate with your energy and intentions.

### AURIC SPRAY

Spritz with intention across any space, including your own aura, to cleanse and uplift the energy.

### ROLLERBALL

Apply with intention directly on your meridians or organs for targeted support and energy balancing.

*Each essential oil bottle has been energetically imprinted with specific frequencies that align with connection and cleansing, enhancing their therapeutic benefits.*
*For questions or assistance with these expansion options, visit www.LetHealthFlow.ca*

## Add manifesting and affirmations to your toolkit

Be Your Own
Cheerleader

One Minute
Manifest

### AFFIRMATIONS

Journey through the process of creating powerful affirmations that will help you believe in yourself and your abilities.

### MANIFESTING

A powerful e-Mini that helps you connect to your heart's desires and bring them into reality in just one minute a day.

# Empowering You

TO DEEPEN YOUR CONNECTIONS AND
TRANSFORM YOUR LIFE, ONE TOOL AT A TIME.
THE POSSIBILITIES ARE ENDLESS, IT'S UP TO
YOU HOW TO USE THEM.

# The Connection Collection

*Experience Connections **to self**, community and beyond*

*The Connection Collection* is a powerful set of programs designed to help you dive deep into the energy of connection for greater self-awareness and personal growth.

This collection provides a wealth of resources to help you stay focused and motivated on your journey toward greater connection and consciousness. Whether you're looking to break free from old patterns or cultivate a deeper sense of connection in your daily life, this collection has something for you.

## The Connection Experience

You are invited to explore the power of connection for self-awareness and personal growth. Whether you're looking to improve your relationships, manifest your goals, or simply connect more deeply with your inner wisdom, *The Connection Experience* can help you tap into the power of connection and use it to create positive change in your life.

## Your Connection Experience Notebook

A guided companion for *The Connection Experience*, providing space to record thoughts, quotes, and affirmations to support your journey towards greater self-awareness and connection.

## The Connection Cleanse

A transformative experience designed to help you clear negative energy from your life and create space for positive, high-vibrational connections. Through a combination of self-reflection, guided exercises, and energy work, you can release what no longer serves you and open up to the possibilities of what could be.

## The Connection Cleanse Toolkit

A powerful resource designed to help you cleanse and revitalize your energy. It contains a variety of tools and exercises that can help you disconnect from draining connections, and attract positive and uplifting energy into your life.

## One Minute Manifest e-Mini

By taking just one minute to focus your energy and attention on your goals, you can start to attract the experiences you desire into your life. This practice aligns with the teachings of *The Connection Experience*, which emphasizes the power of connection and awareness in creating a fulfilling life.

## Be Your Own Cheerleader e-Mini

Helps you tap into the power of self-belief and positivity to create affirmations that inspire and motivate you to achieve your goals. By infusing your affirmations with positive energy, you can cheer yourself on and accomplish anything you set your mind to.

Visit **TriciaSybersma.com** for more details

# About Tricia

Tricia was born in Toronto, Canada and resides in the Cayman Islands. Her passion for helping drives her to write, speak and mentor others seeking joy, freedom, and unshakable personal power through Gratitude, Connection, and Action.

Being a HeartMath® Certified Trainer, a published author and TEDx speaker, Tricia shares her inspiring and honest vulnerabilities to encourage her readers to be strong. She truly believes that navigating through valuable life lessons, brings new perspectives that invite readers to connect to their heart and live an authentic and fulfilling life.  She has had many of her own opportunities to navigate life challenges with careers, parenthood, living abroad, adversities, as well as healing, and embracing life to the fullest.

*"What truly matters, is how we experience our stories within the world around us. I invite you to step into the flow of Gratitude, Connection, Action to create a field of opportunity for positive change in your life."*

*Tricia Sybersma*

**The Gratitude Experience is a powerful and inspiring book that will transform your life by teaching you how to cultivate gratitude in a mindful way.**

*Learn how to shift your perspective and focus on the positive aspects of your life, even in the face of challenges and difficulties. By practicing gratitude, you'll open yourself up to new opportunities and experiences, and you'll start to see the world in a more positive light.*

*Start your journey of gratitude today and experience the transformative power of this life-changing practice.*

# Join the community

Stay up to date on the newest books, e-minis, gifts and other offerings.

## Email:

Tricia@TriciaSybersma.com

## Website:

www.TriciaSybersma.com

## Facebook:

/Ggnow2015

## Instagram:

/triciasybersma

## Twitter:

/tsybersma1

## RedBubble:

/Tsybersma